Bracing

by

Simone Mansell Broome

The Conrad Press

Bracing
Published by The Conrad Press in the United Kingdom 2023

Tel: +44(0)1227 472 874
www.theconradpress.com
info@theconradpress.com

ISBN 978-1-916966-02-4

Copyright ©Simone Mansell Broome 2023

All rights reserved.

Typesetting and Cover Design by: Levellers

Original illustration for front cover by Cerys Susannah Rees

The Conrad Press logo was designed by Maria Priestley.

Printed and bound in Great Britain by Clays Ltd, Elcograf S.p.A.

Dedicated to

Roger, Matthew, Crispin and Eleanor, thanking Roger especially for his ongoing practical and emotional support.
Thanks are also offered to Cerys Susannah Rees, Louise Weldon, Kay Margerison, Judith Barrow and to everyone who has published me, is about to publish me or has encouraged me creatively over the last few years.

Also by
Simone Mansell Broome

Poetry
Not exactly getting anywhere but...
Juice of the lemon
Cardiff Bay lunch
Getting off lightly (ebook)
A cwtch in Kyrenia

Children's fiction
Valletta and the year of changes

Journal (prose and poetry)
Pause -12 months of going nowhere

Memoir
Falafels, some frogs and a ferret

Contents

Breeze..9
- Digging..11
- Gargoyle..12
- For my daughter's mother-in-law's sister......13
- As kings, in Egypt..................................15
- After the rains return............................16
- A lady novelist writes to a publisher, 1972......17
- Blew in..18
- Vision..20
- When we were first together....................21
- Osculation..22
- Summer shower......................................23
- The pull of the lizards............................24
- Boy, playing..25
- He's a nice lad.......................................26
- Milady fair..28
- St. David's..29
- Not getting my autograph book signed by John Noakes. 30
- Speed awareness 31
- On hold..33
- Hole punch..34
- Lemon cheesecake with ginger................35
- Cancelling God....................................36

Named for the tree..37

Blast..

To my Suffragette...39

The classroom..42

The migration of Bewick's swan.........................44

In the nursery...45

Just a little prick..47

Evergreen...50

Love, house, vinyl, desire....................................51

Polar bear and Oyster..52

Again..54

Last Samaritan in Paris..56

Confession..58

Were you there, bear?..61

It's an ill wind..

52.0136 North, 4.3881 West – 21st February 2022........64

Balance...66

A coffee and a chat - Barmouth...........................67

Springers in the air...68

Like a duck to water...69

A photo for Grandpa...70
Inevitability...71
Celebration..72
Nessun Dorma...73
The visitor..74
January 6th...75
Springing 76
I am becoming all those words 77
Diagnosis..78
Retreat..79
Revelation..81
Checking up on Dad...83
What do we do now?..84
For him there was no longing......................................85
At the bar...87

Acknowledgements.................................88
About 'Bracing' and about Simone...........89

Testimonials
'I thoroughly enjoyed the collection, and hope I conveyed that!'
'Simone Mansell Broome's new poetry collection, *Bracing,* is just what its title promises. These wide-ranging poems emerge from everyday life—a trip to the hairdresser's or St David's, languishing on hold on the phone—and are by turns playful and profound, able in the flick of a line to tether glimpses of resonant meaning to quotidian chores, annoyances, joys... Broome's accessible, down-to-earth poetry faces life as if out for a walk on a windy day, in sensible dress and footwear, shorn of sentimentality. For her, hiraeth is a gust of privilege to which she is entitled but not her father, who was raised in a Wales of duty and hunger, for whom "there was no longing." I highly recommend this poet's sense, sensibility, and hearty companionship.'
Pamela Petro, author of *The Long Field* and *Travels in an Old Tongue.*
'LOVED your collection! So much to think about. You have such an interesting take on your world! Such varied topics from way back in time to now.'

'Well, what a joy your collection has been to read. I had to stop many times to dwell on the conjured images and emotions.'

'Simone writes with great poignancy and humour, sharing her view of moments both observed and imagined. The diverse everyday and unusual are keenly observed. Many poems are sensuous, leaving lingering secret smiles on lips. Each is a gem to savour and revisit. A collection of wonders, no doubt you'll enjoy.'

'Several times I found myself thinking, 'Oh, I wish I'd written that!' Brilliant.'
Jackie Lyndon, Pinewood Press
'Broome's poetry is characterised by candour, wit & close observation. She has an original turn of phrase which is very arresting.'
Mike Jenkins, writer and editor

Breeze

*Poor Winston's idea of foreplay was,
'Brace yourself, Effie.'*
Mrs Doubtfire (1993)

Digging

A single kite circles: it's clear and warm. There'll be
a postcard perfect sunset - not yet. I'm sitting
on a tan plastic chair, the type that stacks, while you
dig. I'm holding a ginger cat. He's a dead weight,
eyes pale, open, no shade I remember.

We grumble, you and I, about rubble buried
under the grass, (the man who lived here before us
making this task so much harder), bluntness of tools -
spades, forks, a bent shovel, a pickaxe - me silent
as you plant a walnut tree beside him.

Six years before, August, morning, this time a dog -
your dog, the other woman we'd joked about, how
I watched from a window, closed, upstairs. Having found
your spot, you laboured amongst and between deep roots.
When all was done, you lay down next to her,

wept, and the rawness of it hooked me back once more.
Tonight I've untied the 'missing' notes from railings:
the lone kite's back - he pauses, plummets, banks, then soars,
circles and keens, circles and keens.

Gargoyle

Some say he looks like my husband, benign,
a little playful, meaning well as he watches
from his aerial perspective.

He has no name yet. We know he was one of many,
chipped out of the mould, to add a touch of whimsy
to some Victorian house of God

or villa of man. He is a composite creature,
webbed and clawed, with bony spine, a long tail,
of upright ears, bulbous of eye and manic of grin,

yet no malice attends, exudes, can be felt.
While the sculptor in a far barn is making
his one-off, power tooling his ear-defended way

through limestone and Carrera marble,
raising dust, drilling and hammering across
valley, hills. In orange boilersuit.

Hard physical work, noisy toil,
solitary work punctuated by breaks for tea
or cigarette, or by idle enquirer. The artist at work.

For my daughter's mother-in-law's sister

For my daughter's mother-in-law's sister
is a splendid specimen of woman, lady
of a certain age, not old enough
to be at risk, not at leisure and so,
alas, furloughed.

For my daughter's mother-in-law's sister
is fine in style and substance, efficient,
proficient in many areas. No shirker. She is
a grandmother, and she keeps a flat in Hove
with a view
of the promenade.

For my daughter's mother-in-law's sister,
deskbound for decades, now footloose, fancy-free
but for how long? She has signed an official piece
of paper. Latter-day landgirl, she must
make ready, hold steady, join willing ranks
who'll plug the labour gaps
this summer.

For my daughter's mother-in-law's sister
will be a classy fruitpicker, in eyeliner,
bright blue, in cropped white linen slacks, a panama hat,
red painted toenails, practical walking sandals.
Decrees say she is needed; she must dirty her hands
for this country's good.

For my daughter's mother-in-law's sister
must go down to the fields, a trug just hung
carelessly at her elbow. No shirker,
she's a wonderful worker. She will toil
and labour and save the day
this year's harvest.
My daughter's mother-in-law's sister.

As kings, in Egypt

Mother tried to broaden my mind. A jaunt to peer
at dusty objects in glass cases? A Nile trip? Luxor's glories?
I revolted. A callow girl - before love, before marriage,
fifteen short years before Carter opened
the boy king's tomb and all changed for ever. Back then,
I revelled at the Gezirah Palace Hotel, *my court*, with teas,
polo, young men, dances. Belt-tightening banished, bolted
from England's chill dull wintry tomb. *I would return*
to Egypt, fall for that scented heat, muezzin's calls,
the draw of other lives, antiquity, the East.

After the rains return

and children are back in school,
their days circumscribed, filled
with people, vivid with stuff;
and they've stopped playing slip-and-slide,
or in the mud kitchen, or just
endlessly bouncing on trampolines,
will the arrival of eleven chicks still enthral?

New life works its magic, especially
on the young, but more so now.

After the rains return, and blue is scarred again
with the tracks of jumbos,
and birdsong and bleating is fugged
a little more by cars; yet we can hug,
go to the pub, get our roots done,
dive into buzz and bustle, nine-to-five,
full diaries, will we thrill as business beckons?

When 'new normal' is bagged and boxed
for the bin men, will we shrug it off,
slip back?

After the rains return, and news is other
than this plague, will we submit
to gaining liberty, while losing our balance?
When we stop waiting for the when and how,
stop clapping; will we chat and gossip
at the gates, but waste less,
less life,
less time,
after the rains return?

A lady novelist writes to a publisher, 1972

Sirs, you are doubtless aware of the queues,
thousands at our British Museum
these summer months, *Tutmania* raging
once again.
I have unearthed and dusted off this manuscript,
a wild card circa 1937,
even as I toiled, penning *Death on the Nile*...
We surely know what works and what does not,
scene changes too many, cast too vast.
The whole opus uncommercial. I have
no illusions about its stage success.

This Pharoah, he drew me in, husband
of Nefertiti, (father of the boy king
we no longer call *Tutankhaton*
or *Old King Tut*). A serious man
with serious intent, lover of Ra, wanting
to move worship from the many to the one.
Unpopular stance back then.   There is poison too.

By the time of Akhnaton, I knew my place,
what was expected, what would appeal.
But this play of my middle years was born
from interests, passions shared, when my life
was moored by travel, curiosity,
good friends, *not being alone* and hard graft.
Always. My days of wilder sorrow   long past.

He helped, somewhat, but mostly I addressed
all questions to Sidney, *dear Sidney.* Not what fans
have come to expect from this purveyor
of bestsellers, but I wrote to please myself,
not for success. It needs some small sunlit space.
Do publish.

Blew in

Blew in on a new moon he did, blew in
in faded denims, a sweater with holes,
leather patches at his elbows, the craftsman -
much needed, recommended - arrived

as the parish slept, parked up between playground
and the hall where things happen, Art Club, W.I.,
Silver Surfers and Pilates class, the hive
of industry lodged in an Arts and Crafts gem,
smelling of beeswax, community spirit.

He stayed put, despite murmurs, hunkered down
through autumn, winter, spring, worked hard, got
the job done. Not a friend of the way things
were usually done, wanted cash, was not prepared
to compromise on that.

His kind was in short supply.
He was undistinguished in face, frame,
property, power, owning little compared to those
who left at dawn in company cars
bound for flight or train.

All he seemed to have
was his mobile home, the tools he used
in his mason's art and a talent to observe,
to be still, to listen. And the women
of the village noticed him,

tried a little more
before turning out for classes, clubs, school or swings,
found interest in the restoration project.
Even the sensible simpered, wavered, teetered.

That next summer, as the grass grew back where
his home had stood, in flushed, wine-bold huddles
women excused themselves – *but he noticed, he seemed
to understand* –

and even if each knew by then
she was not unique, it was just something he did,
could turn on and off, a trick to beguile
by attentiveness,
her pulse still quickened.

Vision

We're talking about men, the male body,
the young, smooth, chiselled sort, lithe
and muscular, everything in its place
but not too much of it, neither oiled
nor pumped up. Nor orange. I'm thinking
of the Wife of Bath, her appreciation
of a youth's legs, her open fondness
for male flesh. And you're telling me
about your guest, B&B, who wanted the code
for the Wi-Fi, and duly, like a good hostess,
you procured it and tapped at his door.

Finally, your reward came. A vision,
towel wrapped around his taut, damp, belly,
answered, thawed you with a smile, and you say
how, for a moment, you forgot your mission,
forgot that it's rude to stare, stood there, mute
on the threshold, thunderstruck, awed.

When we were first together

She said, rubbing unguents into my hair,
(no longer luscious locks, a flaxen rope,
no, now more a faded halo, static frizz),

when we were first together, we'd walk the dogs
and I'd dawdle, idle, trail behind him, a few paces,
not subjugated, but just so I could stare

at his bottom, all perfect in its pertness. Now
he's got *so* thin, his arse is pancake-shaped. We walk
arm in arm. I ask what she's using on my hair.

'*Loss control*', I find out after but it sounds like
lost control. We roar. My mop's a lost cause,
and, as for control, of me, tomorrow, life - no chance.

In a world, a week, a day packed with sadness,
I think of my man's rear, count blessings where I can.

Osculation

We meet by chance
in the health food shop,
gannets gathering around the last
of today's bread delivery.

The talk, of course,
is all about the weather,
this heat we still find alien,
and the unexpected benison

of a summer shower.
'Come into the garden, Mark,'
she says she said. Apparently,
there have been forty eight hours

of no kissing.
Intimacy too sticky
to bear. So, the woman in front of me,
with her *pain de campagne,*

the unbleached white, rye
and wholemeal sourdough,
and five shiny croissants for the morning,
tells us, the queue,

how *they* revelled
in some luxury
of slow uxorious smooching
in the warm, Welsh rain.

Summer shower

Just now, there were two thunderclaps,
that prescient pause, and then rain.
At first it seemed to be a passing shower,
but we thought wrong. The clouds
unburdened themselves. You drank
your coffee, laughing as I ran to rescue
newly pegged out washing.

These last few weeks, I have become used
to trusting the weather, to trusting the sun
to persist, to trusting that there will be
the smell of line-dried linen come the evening.
What folly! I fumble with unclipping, mocked
by fat, hot, earthbound tears.

Twenty minutes and it's over, but the air
is thick, the sky still laden, my skin sticky.
Outside the kitchen, the decking dries fast. Pets
are on shutdown, eking out energy
in furry torpor. I am a creature

of temperate climes, loving the lusciousness
of a Mediterranean summer, yet
barely able to function when it comes here.
I will need to adapt.

The pull of the lizards

Seen on cartoons, in books, as toys - he knows them all.
Herbivore,
carnivore,
omnivore;
voracious in their appetites; he can say their names,
their terrain of choice, their habits, likes. Their world
fills his games.

This little boy, like many more, he knows them all.
Real creatures stalk his world. They populate
his days, his nights. He likes them mean
and likes them nice. He likes them huge
with an enormous roar. It doesn't matter
that they're extinct, that they're not here now.
He knows they lived and thrived before.

He likes them good but the bad, somehow,
are better, more enticing. He knows their names.
The terrible lizards' pull survives; they fill
the minds of most small boys.

In the games he plays on the kitchen floor, he likes
them huge with a very loud roar. It's safer now
they're not here anymore; those terrible lizards –
who lived and thrived and were fierce once before.
He knows their names-
all the dinosaurs.

Boy, playing

At lunchtime, sausages untouched,
neither sitting nor standing, but
quivering on jack-knifed leg; front teeth,
quite new, clamped tight over lower lip,
frowning like his granddad, his uncle,
before a penalty is taken,
faint humming stirs a straight light fringe.

And that small device, which beeps, has lights,
cannot be prised from nimble fingers
for a wash, for food or drink, for aught
except a clap of exultation,
brief table drumming of his success -
as with those skittering, deft digits,
he scales the heights, his best score yet.

He's a nice lad

You forget he's only twenty seven:
his brow folds, wrinkles, crumples;
there are crevasses you don't recall
before thirty.

He's done well, dropped out somewhere between
GCSEs and the end of year twelve,
finished his education in the school
of board - surf and skate -
then snow.

Majored in minor damage, not doing himself
injuries he couldn't get over,
gaining much on the hop, on the slope,
curve, wave, ducking and diving, carving,
swerving, the turf,

the powder he knew, had dealt with, had always
dealt with. No big deal. No worries.
This latest drama is just a blip,
the past crossing his snowy graph, not worth
breaking sweat,

not worth breathing a word to this girl he's earmarked
as his key to survival, to breaking free
from generations, from history,
from family. He's reinventing, creating
his future,

making that myth where it's all groovy,
where he's in control, has a goal, where the guy

with shifty troubled eyes, a brow too creased
for twenty seven, gets the girl. She's
an ice-queen,

pure and simple, triple a rated.

Milady fair

Milady fair, she packs a verbal punch;
her voice clear, sure, unwavering – views too,
and freely shared. Petite, on small neat feet,
she moves, all camera ready, aware.

She dresses to impress herself, misses
nothing, is swift in reply, or just records,
for leisurely recalling, to deliver
her asides, later, timed for peak effect.

She gives no quarter, has no truck with tact,
flaxen hair flicked as she fixes her victims
with a blistering stare if
exacting standards are not met

to milady's satisfaction. Spares none.
Yet this force of nature can play the clown,
mock herself, act against type,
forget her brand in an instant, with a smile

to unfreeze ice caps, infectious laughter, caught,
of course, on video. Gone viral. Then snaps back,
turns on a whim to critic, examiner, a power
not to be challenged, pure, beyond compare,

milady fair.

St. David's

We've already done a double-take, that cleric
at the path's end. Tall, gaunt, his face obscured,
a grey hoodie shrouding it, sandals, the Jesus sort,
loose grey trousers. Simple mistake to make.
I saw homespun cassock, footsore traveller,
man at the summit of a long, long walk, hunting
salvation. And then he vanishes.

Here, we are tuned in to mystery, wowed by history,
our senses alert to the possible. However many
emporiums for outdoor gear, fashion outlets,
flavours of ice-cream assaulting our eyes, awe still
exerts power. So unassuming today, the sunlit stroll,
a slow incline and then turn right, dip, go down
the steps and *she's there* nestled, cwtched in a fold.

As she's always been. Attended by meadow, wild flowers
nodding approval, roofed by blueness, with stream
beside and sea beyond. There is no shouting, pomp,
display, just the double slope, the smooth floor,
the cool, and always that sense of sinking
into earth, rock, millennia. Poor Gerald, his chances
scuppered perhaps by the Welsh grandmother.

Angharad. You pause to read about Cranmer's death,
flesh melting, too little reform, too much, a dance
that finished in the flames. And now you hear the voice,
earnest, clear, explaining something – doctrine, liturgy,
faith – to two tourists. '*Ultimately,*' he says, '*it depends
on what, and how much, you believe.*' Silent assent
follows. No fires this time. We are ecumenical now.

Visitors, tanned, sparkly, decanted from a ship today,
wander. As we do. A gift which gives each time.
Escape. Renewal. The lightest brush with pilgrimage.

Not getting my autograph book signed by John Noakes

I never had a Blue Peter badge, not one.
I wasn't a joiner-in, a taker-part. And as for Brownies,
though *the plan* was always to get a raft of badges
to buck up the drab, ditch-water brown dress...I didn't.
The pony-trekking trip was also not a success.

Instead I sang, recited, read, my head full of dreams
and stories.

There was a fete, some damp Berkshire village green,
Bradfield, Burghfield or wherever, and he was there,
with his dog. *Was it Patch?* His role was judge,
of pets, paintings, cakes or carrots. Or all of them.
You know the drill. And it poured. We sheltered,

he and I, under damp canvas, while puddle
became lake at the scout tent door flap. We downed
sweet weak tea, did justice to a plate of custard creams,
slightly soggy, past their best, waiting for it all to ease.

Did I request an autograph? *I did not,*
but we talked, and I petted his dog instead.

Speed Awareness

We are all here, ten of us offenders,
and the man whose task today is to make us
more aware of how we drive, how fast we drive,
how long it takes to stop, and why we break the rules.

I'm in the study, the as yet unsorted, unpacked study,
with not enough storage and no order visible. There is
just about a connection. I am reminded why
I have fought shy, despite the pandemic, of readings,

workshops, anything done via Zoom. It looks as though
most of my partners-in-crime are younger. The way
I decide to survive this morning, is to engage, respond
often, quietly, but not draw attention to myself.

I do not want to be put on the spot, just for the signal
to last, the morning to end. Others take a different line.
The youngest is teacher's pet, keen to speak, to please,
to be heard. A sub-group riffs on towing weights. Two men

only want to chat about their tractors. But the two
we can't ignore are the bored boy doing this course
on his phone, wandering off, drifting back,
with large supplies of packaged snacks, crisps, chocolate,

cans of coke, cigarettes, to keep him fed, filled, occupied.
He is not used to sitting still. You can picture him
at the back of a classroom. You can see how
teachers could have found him difficult...

And the woman lounging on a squishy leatherette couch,
a beige couch, beige leisurewear. No pen or paper,

but brushes, combs, clips, an array of hair accessories.
Throughout the morning she undoes, brushes

and restyles her long thick hair, dyed blue and lilac grey,
balayage might be the name, in complex updos,
side ponytails, waves and twists, and at the close,
she tips her head upside down, while she weaves

her locks into tight French plaits for our delight.
With skill and focus. Who knows how much this morning
has done for *her* driving? Our course leader -
lost for words, as are we all.

On hold

The message warns of a ten minute wait, possibly more.
It's been forty five minutes now, on speakerphone,
so the room too can benefit from what you endure,
in the cause of getting on with other stuff, while waiting.

From time to time a jaunty voice suggests you try
the website. Does she think you haven't tried already?
She is trying to distract us, divert us from this misery
by playing 'Greatest Day' every two or three minutes,

and not confessing where we are in the queue, whether
we've progressed, whether there is, in truth, anyone
there. Gary Barlow belts out his prediction that this
might be, could be the greatest day of our lives.

The recording crackles; sound quality impaired. Only
the jaunty voice stays clear. Through pain, through tedium,
we are left just with awareness of time passing,
some joy in irony.

Hole punch

Listen, *clickcrunch*, I don't punch above my weight.
I'm nothing special, me, a decent straight-up-and-down
kind of gadget. I'm a plug-free zone, batteries
not included, not needed; I don't pretend to be
an oil painting or the glamorous one in Viking.
You won't drool over my lines; I have no vavavoom,

no drama of the guillotine, no intricate meshing
of the machine that binds. I'm not a one-off, not first
of my kind. I just do what it said on my box. I have
no airs above my station in that stationery cupboard.
I don't relieve stress...am not a well-strung executive toy
for strung-out achievers; you don't need instructions

or help file for me; idiotproof, user-friendly – take me,
use me as you find me; don't brag to me of Conran
or Alessi; don't look for me in a museum of modern design;
my value won't appreciate. There'd be no point in laying
down a case of me, like a fine wine. Yet, there is a sure
percussive bite to my cut, a tight precision to my
clickcrunch action....parchment, watermarked, used, laid –
Swoon! Watch me carve circles in your smooth,
recumbent rectangles.

Lemon cheesecake with ginger

For one so careful with everything, conscious
of not wasting, of doing without, putting by,
of make-do-and-mend, she was profligate with food.

Spick, quick, sharp of tongue, demeanour, not a looker
even when young, he was her passport to somewhere,
to a better life, to more. From the greyness, from

certainties of grime, the mine, servitude. Of course
she'd love him, dapper and dandy, with quiff,
cravat and a liking for pink gin. He'd set the bar,

and from that moment, no-one in that northern town
came close. And when she fell, he did the decent thing.
She felt blest: she'd caught, but not quite conquered, him.

She'd ground to cover. The path to his heart was paved
with baking, feeding him up and feeding him well.
Once she tells me how four years later, an old flame

came to call, painted, brassy, chancing one last play
for him, with you and your sister, just babes round
her floured pinny. *I bided my time*, she says,

as she makes lemon cheesecake with ginger,
pounding the biscuits, grinding gingernuts
into fine sand with the blunt end of a rolling pin.

I just hoped and bided my time.

Cancelling God

I tell my friend about the wedding reading. Rare
for me now, it's in a church. Church weddings.

*Can you choose what you read? Something secular;
something funny? One of the usual suspects?*

No, I say. *I'll just read what I'm given. It's not
my day, not for me to pick.*

Will God be invited, she asks? *Has he made
the guest list?*

Probably, I say. *Their call, not mine. My role
is just to read whatever they decide.*

I'd be happier, she says, *if he wasn't included.*

But I *can* cope, will be unperturbed in this setting,

wouldn't dream of blocking his entry, not
letting him in.

*I perch on that fence,
never sure enough of his non-existence
to deny the thought that he might.*

Named for the tree

Ever squeamish I've stepped outside my comfort zone,
beyond the relief we have to feel. The end of pain.
Her long life, lived full. But this day, this ritual is my first.

No body. No fuss. An empty box. We remember,
without her, the way she folded, blended, welcomed,
warmed all visitors, from kin to friends to passing strays.

Alert, bright-eyed bird, maker of Welsh cakes, her kettle
always just off boil, her teapot cosied, ready. *Hazel,*
named for the tree, laden with the silent wisdom

of a thousand casual confidences, wearing her prescience
lightly, easy as dust, as flour. No flowers to coat this truth:
she has flown. What's left will now be shared, studied,

dissected, giving to science, as she gave in life.
We'll dwell instead on fragments – on linen pressed
ready for those guests expected, and as yet unknown,

on fresh bread doorsteps sliced, on endless baking,
on days spliced with old observance, throwing salt,
curtseys to a lone magpie, a wooden spoon,
a hazel wand, her span of kitchen kindnesses,
ancient magick.

Blast

Sunshine is delicious, rain is refreshing, wind braces us up, snow is exhilarating; there is really no such thing as bad weather, only different kinds of good weather.
John Ruskin

To my suffragette

The first suffragette hunger strikes began in July 1909. Marion Wallace Dunlop was released after three and a half days' fasting. By the end of September of that year forcible feeding of prisoners was introduced. This procedure carried on till the outbreak of the First World War when the WSPU - the Women's Social and Political Union - called for a temporary suspension of militancy and the government granted amnesty to all suffragettes in prison.

Honey, comfrey and calendula,
arnica, hot beef tea; how can we heal you, make you
strong enough, now the Cat's released its Mouse,
you, home to us, to our house, to me?

I wasn't meant to be their mother, but we do our best
without you, muddle through, suffer the jibes,
the sly asides, the jeers. Sometimes my peers
leave the paper open by a cartoon
of an ugly, strident woman
doing ugly, strident things...
or slide a postcard under the door,
so crude, so cruel and so unkind, I must admit
I hide them from the girls.

Poultice, salve and balm. I'd like to shield you, keep you from
all harm . Hard for a man to see his sweetheart
hated and harangued,
mistreated, manhandled...
Harder still to know, to feel and not to see.
For what women do to property,
man does now to womankind.

*Yet there's no shame for a man who wreaks havoc,
lets go the dogs of war, kills and maims in name
of country, God or cause. No, he's a hero,
of course, garlanded, with honours, statues, property,
acclaim, applauded in epic poem, in songs
of sword and fame, ennobled so his bravery*
carries on from son to son to son,
amply rewarded for Grandpappy's crimes.

But she, maker of fire, destroyer of things made
and owned by man, she's wilful, misguided,
out-of-control, harpy or a whore
or a legion more hateful names.

Deeds not words, the Pankhursts said. *Do not appeal,
do not grovel, do not beg. Take courage, join hands,
stand beside us, fight with us.*

And have you fought, my angel?! You've changed,
grown firmer in resolve, as your body weakens still.
Let me bind you, soothe and comfort you,
clean your cuts, your weals, though your mind's
a stranger to us. Your face hides silent hurts,
secrets left behind the prison door.
Yes, Holloway haunts us day and night.

And that three-colour medal, purple, green and white,
slumped against the mantle clock, while you've been gone again.
Thank God Joan of Arc wasn't married -
that's what I sometimes say, as every time
I get you back, something more of you
has been stripped away, ounces, pounds, stones;
they've taken blood, hair, flesh,
exposed your nakedness.

*It's all for King and country,
how dare you make a fuss,
now the Kaiser's on the warpath,
once again it's 'them' and 'us'!*

We can only stand by, patch up and mend,
expecting the worst, as countless women
have done for countless men.
Our roles reversed.

*Honey, comfrey and calendula,
arnica, hot beef tea,* how can we heal you, make you
strong enough now the Cat's released its Mouse,
you, home to us, to our house, to me?
As for you my battered darling, you're a woman out of time,
before your time, for all time,
right place, wrong time.
They say you choose what you do, but where is choice
when you are voiceless?
Where is choice when you are voiceless,
and when victory comes, where will you be?

The classroom

I'm not sure who thought it wise to put
a small, rookie teacher, aged twenty two,
looked eighteen,
into that North London classroom, packed
with teenage Cypriot boys on the cusp
of manhood, and some already men.

There were Greek and Turkish boys,
similar numbers of each, reluctant
to be there,
not keen on learning anything, fired up
with testosterone, with stoked hostilities.
It was a blistering hot summer.

I was told to keep the windows closed
lest any climb out and escape. I was told
to dress modestly,
but this was a given. No cleavage,
no sleeveless tops, nothing tight,
nothing which might show anything
if the light was behind me.

No to high heels, in case I needed to move quickly,
and no to jeans or trousers
lest they clung.
As for skirts, long, loose but not too floaty, nothing
to grab or catch hold of. I wasn't told how much
I'd need to raise the volume
of my voice.

I wasn't told never to walk amongst them, always
to hand things out, collect things in, *delegate to two*

at the front, one from each camp.
I wasn't told never to turn my back
for more than a second, two at most, to write
on the board.

Handouts were safer. I wasn't told
I'd be ducking missiles launched from anywhere.
We were always seconds from violence,
against each other, against me. I wasn't told
not to show fear.
It was a hot summer.

The migration of Bewick's swan

Night draws in as ice-tipped wings lip Eastern coasts.

And they're fetching you back   West,
demons clinging to your coat tails,
uncertain footholds for the ones who clamour,

while shadowy birds busy, bustle, chatter
on high wires, while bats disband, dive
into eave and chink and cranny.

You thought to throw them off, flee
to mountain, beach, old haunts or even now,
to bland urban scrawl, outer London, bolthole.

Dusk draws in round here by wine-o'-clock, evenings
drowsed through with coaxing of fires, TV murders,
News at Ten and a shrill owl or two.

You thought to shake them off, escape to hills,
the sea, your past or catch an Eastbound train,
your trip a torture of proximities,

uneasy closeness to all those passengers,
travelling hopefully...your plumage bedraggled,
some dulled imperative of flight.

Fetching you back, as some fly voiceless
and you cry 'capture', back West
to the dark months at the year's turn,

while Winter's harbinger, one small perfect swan,
named for the engraver,
brings arctic chill on wings,

ice-tipped,
from the North, the East.

In the nursery

Had heard the cries, noose tightening around your guts,
you know before you know that something's wrong, sense it,
sniff the blood. Basilisk, dingo, dog, bear, fox, wolf,

he's lean and mean and hungry, has strayed into where
he shouldn't be... when the snows drift in and there's no food,
when his old hunting ground's built on and there's no food;

he's padding down alleyways, slipping through back gates,
sneaking a share of your urban space. Now you've got
decking, designer plants in pots: he's bold as brass

and twice as fearless, lurking by the barbecue,
pushing over bins, nicking the bird food, making
mischief, havoc, mess. That smell - flesh, rot, rut, shrieks

at mating, enough for chaos without the rest.
At night when you've crept inside he's there, all stretched out,
devil-may-care, warming his pelt on the hot tub roof...

Had heard those cries, byebabybye, huffing and puffing
up the stairs to where you've told tall tales, by the crib,
of battles of wits...wily Mister Fox, clever,

sly, admire his cunning. And stories of the forest
beasts, wolf in Granny drag, while down by the Tiber
a she-wolf suckles those boy baby twins. You know

how bad it is before you know...bear's come to camp,
ogre's in the cradle. In the dark, we didn't
see him, switched on the light, and he's there. Unflinching

yellow eyes, reflecting the electric. That stare, unblinking. And there's blood in the cot, bye baby bunting; your Daddy's going hunting...again, soon.

Just a little prick

The King is riled – *just a little prick* - a short, sharp kick,
enough to thwart the thrust of his intent, a royal man's attempt
to plug the dyke, as is his right, to master this event,
take hold of these   *celebrations.*

Beauty – *tick*; brains – *tick*. A pliant nature, sweet, low voice,
kindness, an air of grace, endowed with virtues womanly.
The first six fairies meet the court eye to eye, rank to rank;
no curtseys, heads unbowed. Speak your piece, bequeath
your blessings, so much, so good, so as you'd expect. Rock
the cradle, not the boat. *Tick.*

The King is narked, for after all, he's listened to advice,
the Chancellor, the Dowager...he's toned it down, reined in
the scale: he's ousted God, some smarmy priests. What's left?
No christening party but instead, secular naming rites,
with guestlist trimmed, curated, ecumenical, a boutique,
bijou range of the politically correct, the worthier gift-givers.

The seventh fairy sidles up with four more – the rebels,
the alternatives. No well-groomed gloss, no sparkle here.
Defiant deliverers – *a pepper spray, loud whistles,*
shrill alarms, bright torches to light and hopefully deflect
assailants, crash course in self-defence.
The King is shocked. Surely not! We're talking
of his only child, his pride and joy,
(though not a boy), the gently snoring hostess
at this still gilded bash.
What need of protection has this blue-blooded babe?
Would anyone dare harm one hair of Aurora's head?

'Around the clock security, 24/7, hordes

of burly henchmen, all tight and shiny suited, jackbooted,
on red alert. My daughter's sacrosanct, secure.'

A hush descends. Pins drop. White faces reflect crystal
chandeliers. One fairy's heard to mutter:

'Other parents thought the same,
but now it seems, princess, peasant, whore or crone,
we're all fair game. Wise up King;
safety's a myth, a will o' the wisp.
We're all at risk.'

Into tainted air the twelfth one speaks. Bad fairy's curse,
the cruel hex?
Just a little prick, a point of pin, needle, spindle
drawing the blood of a sixteen year old girl.
The ballroom freezes. Someone faints. Only the brambles
and the rose with thorns, only these move; only these begin
to grow. The King despairs. The fairy speaks,
this time loud, this time clear.

'One hundred years,' she says, 'not a sentence of death,
but simply of slumber, a benign spell, broken only
by a bridegroom's kiss,
a prince of course.'

There is a palpable sigh of relief. Sleep, yes, not death.
And a wedding to look forward to, feasting and the status quo.

It's now the muttering fairy who takes the floor.

'You're missing the point. A hundred years
may be long enough. When she wakes up you might dispense
with the device of handsome princes? Weddings...
are all very well,

but do you really want your daughter bound to dwell
for life with a man whose only assets are a pleasant face,
and a sword for slashing brambles?
You've heard far worse.
This is no tragedy: no curse.

While your kingdom sleeps, while fairies reign,
the world may turn. You may have learned. You could wake safe.
Invoke the power of magic. Rock that boat.
Wake changed.'

What's a little prick?
What's a little sleep?
What's a hundred years?

Evergreen

Holly, ivy, mistletoe, bring in
the winter. Evergreen to deck the halls,
festoon mirrors, wind up the stair. Paint
it greener, pack the air with scents of pine,
light a fire, candles too, crafted from
our garden hives. Make our Yule full -
natural. And, on the stove, star anise,
cinnamon, cloves, steeping in a pan
of wine. *It was never thus.* Make it so.
Myths to fill these blackest days.

Love, house, vinyl, desire

End of the eighties when they flogged the vinyl,
catalogued it, typed out the list, for sale - a quid
or one pound fifty... that house deposit kitty...

...quite a stash, his
and hers, not much cash - final tally, but this trial
was a sign of their belief in this-is-for-keeps,
record shedding, necessary, see as above.

Polemic, gentle or acid-fuelled, those ones they
still knew all the words to - absurd - had hummed or sung
to, that mourned loves they'd lost, not wanted to lose,
choices foisted on them that they'd not wanted

to choose, fire, doom and gloom they'd clung to, more downs
than ups, highs, lows and blues, pre-compromise times,
festival wellies, dancing shoes, barefoot, bra-less,
dosh- and car-less, some mystery discs that neither

could admit, own up to owning, anthemic,
iconic, charting separate histories. They pruned
most duplicates, parting with unmarked covers, no

handscrawled names, aide-memoires for tardy borrowers,
without message from friend or lover, sold more than
doubles, what's left now rests untouched, a spare bedroom
bottom shelf, here now, another house, other lives.

They sold their vinyl, for whatever they could get,
the culling of baggage, without looking back,
Forever More - words on black plastic...

show some emotion - that's Joan Armatrading;
Bob Dylan - desire; Bob Dylan - desire.

Polar bear and oyster

We gawped at caged creatures, torn from their homes.
Even though we worried about the wellbeing
of inmates, about the ethics of their captive state, zoo
remained a regular haunt, an easy place

to take the kids, to roam with motley visitors.
My favourite, from when *my breeding programme*
started, while my centre of gravity shifted
daily, was the polar bear enclosure. What pulled

me back was an awful attraction, an itch to trap
and gnaw at, a deep sadness for the bear who paced.
His name was Misha, a circus survivor: so the repetition,
the troubled pattern to his tortured days

was, we told ourselves, due, in part, to the life
before his *rescue,* not just to the concrete glacier
upon which he found himself. The size of his gaol,
its gulag awfulness, the dull grey whiteness of his pelt...

it all appalled us yet again we went, drawn back,
as if to check whether something might have changed.
It never did.

In hospital aged sixteen, just a couple of months,
with a bunch of other lost adolescents. We were floundering,
gaoled for our own protection, and all united in shock
witnessing hourly, daily, constantly, the boy who rocked
and keened. So deeply in it seemed he'd never find
a way back out. So with Misha, the polar bear,

far from cuddly, glowing polar white, from thick soft fur,

from home, from snow, from ice, so far from everything
we knew was right.
On my twenty fourth birthday the roving, interesting aunt
sent me a watch – *you'll see time differently
when the baby comes* – she wrote. It was a Rolex Oyster,

small, not showy. I think she was gifting her possessions.
She owned a lot, but maybe had a brief issue
with liquidity. Maybe not. When the baby came,
I did not see time. The watch slipped off my slender wrist,
fell in with the polar bear, smashed.
We found a keeper, went back. There was no trace.

I've never had a Rolex since nor seen another polar bear
incarcerate.

Again

She sees the signs, looking the other way at first,
finding useful work in the sorting of cupboards,
boxing up of toys belonging to a child long
gone, living away, the washing out of fridges:

she's feeling tired to the soul and teeth of her,
but points the finger at hard work, trips up and down
to Mum, an eye script due for changing.

She knows he's listening to voices, eavesdropping
hostile plots, moving away from her, retreating:
he's sure once more she's part of that plan to tap the phones,
shift condiments with menace, infiltrate the news,

and there'll be no catching up with a good night's rest:
night, day, dawn, dusk, not a heartbeat apart,
with the wakeful one wondering

if she can do it, all, again.

He sees the signs,
looking the other way at first, distracts himself
with the slates that slipped in recent storms, finds useful
work in getting down to tax returns, to the gearbox,

haircut, estimate, figures rearranging themselves
on his screen, others just appearing, unbidden:
he's feeling tired to the soul and teeth of him,

blames the stressful time he's had, stomach cramps,
the dodgy hip, perhaps he's overdoing it, should
cut back...but she's startling again when he enters

a room, nursing her phone when she takes a bath,

wearing her remoteness scarf, accessorised
with panic, and the one left watchful's wondering
if he can do it, go through it, all, again.

Last Samaritan in Paris

Rene Robert, a Swiss photographer famous for his images of Spanish flamenco stars, died in January 2022, in Paris, after a fall.

Nine hours.
Not stripped, robbed, beaten this time. Not left
at the side of the road that runs
from Jerusalem to Jericho.
Left for dead. Not this time.

This was
urban abandonment, half a world,
two millennia away. Nine hours
on a cold January night, between
the Place de la Republique and les Halles,
a route he knew well, his bedtime stroll,
his territory.

A dizzy spell,
a trip, a slip, a fall and a man is down,
alien, anonymous. These priests and Levites
tonight are again too busy, too wary to bend
to check. *Look the other way, cross over,
pass by, lost in our own concerns.*

It takes another *invisible* one
to call at last for aid, (maybe another
of those six hundred who'll die
on France's streets this year).
Help comes too late.

If we'd had time,
had known his fame, weighed up the passion
of his art, would he have seemed at last
like one of us?

No ass or inn this time.
Just absence, indifference.

Confession

Forgive us Mother, for we have sinned.
There's no health in us. Nor here on earth.
We dressed up chimps, pinky fingers,
china cups and saucers, used them to sell tea.
It is what it is.

Remember Johnny Morris doing
animal voices? *You saw it too?* We all
went to zoos back then, our consciences
just mildly pricked by small enclosures

for bigger beasts, or if they seemed distressed.
Safari parks, sea-life shows, tricks with dolphins,
whales, seals. *How were we to we know?*

And circuses, yes, *our childhoods* and not
now. A treat 'til the clowns came.
We were where we were. We could bury
our heads in sand, or hang them in shame.

Is it wrong to have ridden camels
in the desert dust? Is it wrong to have seen
those photo monkeys, not stopped that hustle?
Awareness shifts. *Things change.* In our defence,

Earth, our crimes were of ignorance.
Our parents too weren't to know that modern,
new and up-to-date wasn't always best.
There was talk of silent springs but no one

listened, and the few who did were
killjoys, hippies, dinosaurs, while we rushed

careless to a silent summer, silence
of no seasons, all seasons, an absence

of birdsong, bee buzz, broken only by the beat
of wildfires crackling, the lapping of water rising,
nearing all we own, hold dear...

*buy it ship it fly it spend it wrap it in plastic
buy more don't mend it out of sight
and out of mind heading for extinction
but we didn't want to know it*

Now ignorance is no excuse. *We know.*
Don't blame King James - that word in Eden -
dominion. Adam was given power,
lordship, the works. Top dog or top man.

The boss of all creation. But, it's a matter
of interpretation. Something got lost
in translation. Custodianship had obligations,
never just a licence to kill, abuse, destroy,

treat earth as a commodity, a toy. *Confess.*
What we took lightly is troubled, precious,
rare. Cherish songbirds, hedgehogs, mountain hares -
all that dwindles... *We have made it so.*

And the names for things are shrinking too, slipping
from our young ones' tongues - sad irrelevancies.

We cannot mend the planet with a song.
We cannot heal her wounds by play or clay or paint,
or soothe this beaten earth with serenades or prose.
We can't repair what's wrong, make it work again,

can't change the course we've taken, can't undo
the hurts.
What can art do then? It can connect, bind,
remind us we are part – to coin a movie –
of that circle of life. There's no time for despair.
Accept what's done. *Confess* we've been reckless;

we've poached, trafficked, maimed, painted
our faces with stuff trialled on rabbits,
and all the while kept spending, burning, using.
This is huge. This is biblical.

We have made it so. Blame and Hail Marys
won't unmake it. Nor will art.
Yet it's a start. *Confess.* Make art and do
something. Start small.
Start now.

Were you there, bear?

Where? Was it you who lurked in the shadows
of that room upstairs, behind the door, between
the carved brown wardrobe and a chair, dressing gown
slung on its back and clothes folded ready,
for tomorrow? Your eyes, it seemed, were everywhere.

They glared from wallpaper faces, trapped in shafts
of landing light, or between those threadbare curtains
which didn't quite close. You'd set up camp, built your lair
under our beds, ready to snap at cold, bare toes,
catch small ankles unawares. *We loved our bears,*

the cuddly, funny, companion sort, Poohs
and Paddingtons – and the rest. We gave them names,
stood them *foursquare* on pairs of furry feet, made them
speak. But not the one with garish trousers! No.
Rupert scared you. And outside, the real ones – beware

the lines around the squares, or dare, if you're brave,
to probe the darkness of the woods or under the stairs.
Hold your breath; make a wish; say a prayer. You might
stay safe. There could be snares. While all the time,
you're shown those pictures, told those tales

of bears in chains, dancing bears, bears to gawp at,
marvel, stare. Look how tall this one stands, how long
the claws, sharp the teeth, coarse the hair, deep the pelt...
and how this one paces in despair. Night and day. Day. Night.
Au contraire, *delightful stuffed, or what a soft, thick rug*

he'll make! Now South they swim, their world in thaw, seals
somehow rare. Bear - forced to share a shrinking world,

(a world less white), to scavenge, steal, forswearing fear of humans. Unwary bear, pursued by hunger. Thief, pest, threat. *Surely we've got bears to spare.*

Exit bear. The air is seared with gunshot.

It's an ill wind...

When we pulled out into the winter night and the real snow, our snow, began to stretch out beside us and twinkle against the windows, and the dim lights of small Wisconsin stations moved by, a sharp wild brace came suddenly into the air. We drew in deep breaths.....before we melted indistinguishably into it again.
F. Scott Fitzgerald

52.0136 North. 4.3881 West - 21st February 2022

A whiff of Hitchcock on the wind, a dash
of Cary in the new, fast river below us.
This place, this planet, here, now. Franklin
wheels across the valley, clutches the hem
of Eunice's kagoule. Three storms in one week.

Is this the way it's going to be?
The new weather norm. Luckier than some
we've been. No power cuts, not yet; the internet
still works. Friends text about trees down, which routes
to take when you venture out, colour-coded warnings,

a change from the to-and-fro of swapping moans -
trying to make a real appointment
with a doctor, how much more things cost.
And who's had, or got, Covid. On the radio
there's endless squabbling about *rules* and *sleaze*,

shot with news of other storms brewing, crisis
in Ukraine. Back home, we focus on the little things.
A stray trampoline billows, spins, tumbles
towards the water. Beasts are skittish too.
Today, earlier, fifteen renegade sheep

pressed muzzles to my kitchen door, now a wall
of sticky glass. Then moved on; destination
unknown. Up the lane, a gate springs open.
Two donkeys escape. More mayhem in the village:
liberated rabbits, hutches and runs
upended - bunnies startled by sudden freedom.

My man's unfazed, up on the roof, assessing
the damage. *He'll be careful,* he says.
Tomorrow, Tuesday, it's all the twos day,
a date to celebrate. I may bake a cake,
and dream of summers like we think they were
before all this. The storms, the change, this place.

Balance

You've always been the action man:
as for me, I've been the wuss.
Our seesaw tips, next bounces down;
a wobble, a waver, wine-bolder,
braver…then springs back to those *normal* dynamics
of me and of you, of us.

A coffee and a chat - Barmouth

We are two men, two women, two dogs
in the beach-front garden of this holiday hotel,
a dismal but handy place to meet.

We drink four coffees sip by sip. An hour, no more,
of chit-chat, this-and-that, with an in-law
we don't know well. Never will now. And the partner

we know even less. We are here, bound
by our love for the wife of our son. Six lives
and one of us is so close to the end it seems
his skeletal frame has become a thin place,
no longer with us, but not yet gone.

The elephant in the garden crashes around,
careering into tables, chairs, knocking over
water bowls. I am appalled. *He* seems resigned,
letting life slink away. Inside, I'm shouting about
not going gentle. Outside, silent complicity

as we fall back on trivia. We part.
It's the last time we'll meet. So, rush down
to the sea, the sun, walking the dogs.
We have too much to do...to drink coffee
with ghosts.

Springers in the air

'Springers in the air,' the tea towel says
in sloping cursive script. Punning for fun.
The perfect gift from one dog-lover
to another.

The image does it all:
blue skies, plumped-up clouds – a glorious chaos
of canines running, almost airborne,
with helicopter tails and ears like wing flaps...

High days, holidays, special gatherings:
you try to save it for best, lest the brightness
be dimmed, the pattern fade, but it finds
its way back to the rest, the regular stash,
heart of kitchen action.

'Springers spring about,' the young guy says,
owner of a half-grown sprocker, but your dog
is prone, splayed, soaking up bone-warming rays,
sunning the shell of himself,

>at the outmost edge
>of all his springing days.

Like a duck to water

You almost didn't make it, just out of view
of the humans who sat, chatting, downing cups
of tea, amused by a clowning puddle of pups,
tussling and tumbling on new Spring grass.
You scrambled up a ramshackle pile of bricks,
stacked against a plastic butt, and somehow must
have toppled in.

Alarmed by sounds of splashing, we found *you,*
doggie-paddling in blissful unschooled circles, ears
dipping, skimming then skirting the murky surface.
You learned fast – this first watery mishap
changed into a story, your story –
the claiming of that aqueous element
you made your own.

Adventures in, on, across, through water
populate our memories of you. Your chest built
for swimming, ears spread wide, steady, bubbly breathing:
your pelt liquified. Sometimes we'd panic, light failing,
scanning the horizon or bank, and no dog visible.
Would you get washed away, tire and drown
or simply carry on,

forget to turn, your easy strokes pulling you
out into the Irish Sea, to the sunset,
West?

A photo for Grandpa

He'd snapped them all - his choice of verb, not mine -
Queen Mum, Princesses Margaret...and Anne, stars
of chart and catwalk, the rich, the famous
and the bad. Now here he was, winding down,
in a modest studio close to us.

The natural choice for our task.
A *happy families* snap for Grandpa.
The op had gone well: we were told he'd make
a full recovery, yet Grandpa was beset
by gloom, could not face the world, had turned
his chair to the wall.

We were asked to stay away, give him space, so,
having summoned, drilled, scrubbed our wayward brood,
we posed...awkwardly, *the first and only time,*
for this. An image with a large remit,
to tell him that he's loved, that life is good,
that his son's made it, that grandkids scrambled
on the cusp of adulthood.

Things were glossed over, touched up, edited out:
the scene was staged. Not all was rosy
but did it work? Grandpa's chair did turn back round.
No visitors signs were packed away. He caged
his demons, rallied, even as reality
unravelled, soundless, at the edges of our frame.

Inevitability

What's this fixation still with that fourth month?
Instead, pick January while she gawps both ways,
but always dark, slow, cold, bleak. And don't speak
to me of rain...The Kings have been now, done
their thing, and all stars, their star, are blotted out
by cloud, fog, sleet and streetlights. Back inside,
the woman touches lippie up, brushes
her hair, scrolls through her phone. Once more, somehow,
sap begins to rise. We breed. We breed.

Celebration

No, no dessert thanks , we'll have the bill now -
one Californian pizza, extra-large,
half with chillies, (they left them off until reminded).

we've been to a birthday meal; he wasn't there,

two calzones, garlic mushrooms, goat's cheese,
house salad, small, elderly, tired, no dressing
till we ask her, gap-toothed girl with willing smile,

then a pot of scarlet goo arrives, 'red French dressing'
she calls it, bringing juice with lemonade
for nursing mother, two Peronis, one so-so glass

of warm white wine, high levels of noise
so no-one can hear the baby cry. The lights go out
and we get a Happy Birthday blast down by the bar,

cake, sparklers, helium balloons tied to cream curled ribbons,
followed by Cliff's 'Congratulations'. Everyone sings,
for everyone loves a celebration. *We've been*

to his unlocked flat and he's not there. Maybe he's lost
his phone as well as his key, so we're taking it
in turns to ring, to text, to jiggle his infant niece,

taking it in turns to go outside to look, just in case.
Whatever the twist in the plot this time, we'll be
at fault. No, no dessert, thanks, we'll just have the bill.

We've been to his birthday. He wasn't there.

Nessun Dorma

He's a man now; doesn't kick or pass,
dribble or play a ball any more,
toe to foot to knee to head, his love
of the game faded away.

Thought it would last always, thought the years
of sunlight and wellness would last too,
restless infant gone, substituted
by a gilded child – football, success –

team, school, friends then girls. Thinking of him
then, bloodied knees, a ball, I recall
those opening bars, Nessun Dorma,
that old *ice* music working its spell,

pulling the crowds, despite gondoliers,
usherettes' trays, triteness of old TV ads,
overplaying, overworking, over-hyped,
in that time before Diana went, Luciano too,

when Pav was fab and football was king,
when the blue-eyed boy was beautiful,
his demons checked, *ice* music, football anthem,

music of hope, limitless possibility.

The visitor

Having seen him for three days, you thought
he was a fixture here, maybe a stray
who slept in that cave behind the concrete steps,
or a wild spirit, loosely bound by ties of bowl,
food and shelter to a *mostly* empty flat
in town, but *mostly* roaming free.

Each morning now you look from your balcony,
scanning the beach for a busy wet spaniel,
black-and-white, who swims in circles, without purpose,
or for purposeful pleasure, next follows
the sand's arc, makes his usual stops, inspects
each small lawned square of loungers with umbrellas,

white plastic tables, cruises all outer tables
at the awning edges by the two bars,
for the just-in-case, the somethings left,
the serendipitous scraps – a holiday-maker
maybe missing his pet, proffering leftovers.
And then he's back to the water, morning

and evening. His patch, his route, his routine.
But today you've not seen him. Your view, the beach,
the sea, seem empty. Your visitor has gone.
Unease gnaws the inside of your cheek. You have
no way of knowing

January 6th

It's the thirteenth day of Christmas. The swans
have long stopped swimming; those geese ceased laying too,
and as for our assorted lords, ladies,
ordinary mortals – they've all hung up
their leaping, dancing shoes. Musicians have downed
their tools - pipes, tabors, lutes and flutes - and the drums
are stilled. Both the Lord of Misrule and the fool
are sent packing. Yule is done. Twelve days of brightness
in the gloom, and then the kings pop in to the pub,
with some nonsense about stars. They give gifts,
do their royal thing. We send them on their way,
and we're back to winter's dark, to January rain,
as the rain rains every day – we are, you know, in Wales.

It's hard to smile in winter, cakes and ale,
not bread and water. Hard, but we ought... to
see that days already grow longer, nights shorter;
green shoots push through. Deep in the forest,
sap rises. In untended gardens, earth turns,
warms, moves. Leaves will come back; birds will sing,
build nests. World never sleeps. And trees, yes trees.
They remember everything.

Springing

Those first signs, unmistakeable, inevitable
as death and taxes. Catkins of hazel,
more light each day, promiscuous ranks of budding bulbs,
the rarer snowdrop, storm-blasted crocus,

that wilful daisy who ignores all seasonal instructions
and flowers all year. Sap's rising
and I'm not ready: I'm out of step. My rhythms unsynced
with the thrust from the earth's crust,

the urge to bloom, thrive, mate, breed, this drive
for Spring to burst through and delight.
A birthday looms; a child bleeds again;
a crazed puppy is wild with moon, wind, spring...

destruction inside, demonic desire for escape.
Ecstatic tail-thumping escape. But it's all of this
and none of this. Sap's rising and I'm clagged down
on our sodden, boggy path, mired

in post-Covid gloom, striving to reclaim my brain
from February fug, shrug off my guard,
find enough breath for the forwardsonwardsupwards push
of March.

I am becoming all those words

I am becoming all those words I've refused to use,
the ones whose truth I deny...
What's in a number? I have fallen again.

And now the peak flow tube, the box
it came in, (from Boots), the shiny book
of graphed paper in which I'm meant
to make my marks, a dot in biro bookending
each breathing day,

two freshly unpacked inhalers... for now
I have put away all these things, fixing just
on the bruise and swell of ribs, my ribs,
which permit only the most perfunctory
in-out, in-out.

No proper rise and fall, no deep inhale,
exhale of air. It hurts to breathe,
hurts to move. There will be no filling
of lungs, no therapeutic stretch
of my airways.

           Ever the steady one, it was others
who courted danger, worshipped speed,
who hurled themselves up and down
mountains, rivers, rapids, roads, while I – waited,
watched, holding my breath,

fretting enough for the feckless ones.
I have fallen again: I am becoming
those words.

Diagnosis

Three or four bottles into the evening,
post-theatre supper with old friends,
the kind you don't meet up with often
but, when you do, it's like you saw them
yesterday: and you've done politics,

the kids, the state of the planet, had
some hilarity, some banter after all those...
those extremes of on-stage emotion, your friend
starts weeping, wild, raw sobbing in the ladies,
all restraint gone. *A diagnosis.*

And it's unjust, premature, final, cruel.
Nothing will ever be the same between
you all, and everything, the catch phrases,
the not using our names any more,
the same old anecdotes – it all makes sense.

Even the last time, when he drove round
  the roundabout the wrong way,
and no one said *a word.*

Retreat

Here all eat well, except for the one
who rearranges food on her plate,
but copies down the recipes
in classic copperplate
and something close to fervour.

They appoint a monitor to feed and tend
the fire, while disparate groups dissect
house moves, changes of career...and more,
and the yoga teacher recommends
a pillow to support the neck,
align the spine, silk pillowslips
for skin and hair.

It's not cold, she says,
stroking the demonstration model,
and it avoids complexion crumpling.
Chat ebbs and flows. A pop star's wed again.
How does he find the energy? A woman yawns, flicking fast
through pages of 'Hello'. Her sofa partner
is off on shoes and ankle boots, sartorial floss.
There is no reply

but all sit up, attend and watch when one tells
tales of her South Africa trip, at forty,
the search for a surgeon,
how she quizzed three, as you're meant to do,
asked each what they'd suggest;
how one drew so many lines on her she froze,
fled his rooms;

how another asked 'what kind d'you want?
The sort that prompts people to stare, gasp, ask
for details of the man who wielded the knife?
Or do you just want them to say how well you look?'
She chose him.

There is chitchat about
experimental psychology, a little riff on cheese,
the rain, today's walk, last night's sleep, last night's dreams.
But mostly silence,
an unlocking, an unwinding,
a breathing in...deeply.

Revelation

Hard to square his eco-credentials
with love for this beast purring, replete for now
with highest octane food, E5,
temperamental, tricky, a delicate constitution but such
a party animal, smile-bringer, joy-giver.

He recycles assiduously, reuses, upcycles,
buys second-hand, preloved. We both do.
Never happier than when trawling through
charity shops, discovering unloved
or forgotten treasures. He finds it hard
to buy new, boycotts peat, spends Easter Sunday

rescuing an old steel bath, painting it, filling it
with stones and earth and compost,
prior to planting. He buys local, supports
small businesses, small shops, local artisans
and artists. Gave up meat forty years back,
has almost joined me, significant other,
on the vegan path.

He's planted trees, thousands, gave up
long-haul flight, flying, rarely flies – the last six years ago.
Has one rescue dog and one who isn't,
a rescue cat, two rescue sheep, and is thought to be
an all-round good guy...

Yet his love of old things, of vintage and veteran,
extends to engines, motorbikes and cars, especially,
but not just, the British ones. Things well-made, things made
with love, these make his heart beat faster,
lift his spirits, make his soul sing, not just

speed but engine roar, the feel of tyres hugging the road,
the line taken round a bend, his senses on full alert,
the wind, the sun, the light...creature
of contradictions, contrasts, compromise.

I acknowledge his joy, his bliss,
his pure *elation* as the *rev* counter climbs.

Checking up on Dad

You needed to see it for yourselves - the last time
wasn't *so* bad, after all. You'd taken him out
to eat. He'd had some, spilled his half of shandy,
seemed pleased at news of next year's wedding.

When you drove him back, he'd not asked you in.
You could live with that. You put it down
to tiredness, left. If not content, satisfied.
Duty done. *Now* there've been calls, texts. The door barred

to the lady who pops in to check and clean.
He's not left out washing; been absent, missed.
So you go. Just three weeks, not the normal four.
He seems thinner. Uncombed, unshaved, unwashed.

The flat's neglected: the fridge bare. An air
of quiet decay, despair. You find a shirt,
sweater, coat, go with him to buy food. The pub lunch
offer gets rejected. Instead he lets you

make poached eggs. Toys with them, is tearful,
trembles. When you try to shift the topic
from scolding him or fretting, he slips back
half a century. Those early rose-lit days

of marriage. On the trip home, *unsaids* choke
the car. At last, you turn in, stop. Your man looks away,
clears his throat.

He can't remember Mum. He's mixed her up
with the wife before, the one who died
at twenty four. Twelve months, they had. That's all.
It's just not fair. That's what hurts the most.

What do we do now?

The deities have gone, faith's
a fuzzy memory, filled
with buffoons, dodgy clerics
and the frankly misguided,

stranding us secular, alone
with no succour, familiar ritual
for comfort. *'Our thoughts are with you'*
sounds so lame, but thinking of you

is what I've done, have been trying to do
yesterday, today too, between
the broken water main, the burying
of my ancient cat, canvas saturated

beyond the point of no return,
a weeping bride, a tricky mother
of the groom, weather defying
all forecasts. *I did try.*

Some might call it biblical,
a scourge on unbelievers,

a plague on climate deniers.
Let me lighten the day

with laughter at lunchtime, secrets
shared over glasses of wine, since
there is probably only now, Prosecco
and friendship, only now and love.
God's keeping a low, very low profile:
you might say he's left the building.

For him there was no longing.

For him there was no longing. The past was
mostly nasty, brutish, cold and poor. Love
absent, or at least curtailed, after TB
claimed his mother. In his Wales, in his childhood,
hunger gnawed at the cottage door. Nothing
was secure, sure any more. A sense of duty -
needing to reduce the tally of mouths
needing to be fed, backs to be clothed, feet
to be shod - that sense pressed hard.

And yet, I did hear tales of Tenby swims,
moonlit dives from the rocks - he bore the scars -
covering up for his elder sister's forays
with boys, pranks at school, usually with fire
or explosions, always rewarded by cane.
And there were anecdotes, stories, roughly drawn
characters recalled, regaled from the front seat
of a small car as we drove back. Because we did -
come back, again and again.

His sibling bonds were deep, strong even though
the flow between those who left and those who stayed
was wide, unnavigable, each side bewildered
by the other.

His Wales was one of missed opportunity,
narrow minds, affection denied to a child. His Wales
cut short his schooling. In Narberth he chose French,
not Welsh, and if it's not too big a stretch, I'd say
his feelings about France, the French, things French,
language and culture, these - though unspoken
to me - were close to *hiraeth* for him.

And we, his daughters, could stay at school, get

degrees, all trace of accent chipped away
by well-meaning nuns. His voice was rootless,
precise, with just a trace of lilt when moved
or riled.

He found it strange, our love for a Wales
we barely knew. Of course there was family -
aunties, cousins, a welcome which embraced us,
but the getting here was long and grey, grey towns,
rain, the sweet sulphurous smell, decaying
industry, *so many chapels*. And even
after they built bridges it was as if the gods
were punishing us for coming back, coming home.

I think with me it was going West, it's always been
going West I anticipate the keenest. All stirred up
with bits of past, Tenby, the sea, the hills beyond,
my parents' friends in some sunny idyll
where I am held, safe, loved and yet a witness,
an observer.

Fiction, myth, but I longed for it without knowing,
and travelling West, I felt quickening.
Even coming back for funerals,
there was something about mourning, something
about music, something about loss -
it was *better* here. Wales did it better.

It's changed now. I've been here sixteen years:
I am home and the longing is silent but not quite gone.
My Wales is not the Wales my father felt. My Wales
is an old Wales, a land that hasn't lost its soul,
and when I leave, and then return, there is still
the pull, the pulse, the flush, the heartbeat,
the sense of a chasm closing.

For him, there was no longing:
for me, it was never a 'whether' but always a 'when'.

At the bar

I bought a stash of sympathy cards, he said,
got them knocked down, cheap. Ones with rhymes
and ones without. I keep them in a drawer.

He's maybe twenty years my junior. Perhaps more?
He's on a riff, a roll. Is he trying to be funny?
Gallows humour at the bar. I part my lips

and bare my teeth, trying to play along.
You can never have too many! He's served
at last. As he moves away, I feel relief.

I don't want mourning to be the norm, don't want
to plan for grief. Tell me about babies, how much
they weighed. Give me details – don't be brief.

Who's moved in and who's moved out, whose house
sold in a day, new schools, jobs, holidays. Let me
congratulate you, celebrate with you, wish you

well, or many more. Fill me in on family feuds,
wedding plans, and pets. You can even share
the news of speeding tickets, parking fines,

driving test success. This isn't denial. I know
how it all ends, how life is troubled, short, cursed,
but my survival depends on not anticipating,
not expecting the worst. I have no time

to stockpile cards. Instead, I cherish life;
spend it well and spend it fast.

Acknowledgements

Some of these poems have been published in ezines, magazines and websites including Reach, Littoral Poetry, Dreich, Red Poets, Wildfire Words, Country Living and The Aberystwyth Ego, in anthologies including 'Smoke and Mirrors', 'Red Lamp, Black Piano', 'A Star fell from Orion', 'Poems for the Year 2020' and 'Gwrthryfel/Uprising', an anthology of radical poetry from contemporary Wales. A few poems appeared in my lockdown blog, which later evolved into *Pause – 12 months of going nowhere* in late 2022.

Four were commissioned for performance - 'Just a Little Prick', 'Confession', 'To my Suffragette' and 'For him there was no longing', for which thanks are due to The Seagull Gallery, Cardigan, Ann Fletcher-Williams and Attic Theatre, Newcastle Emlyn. Two poems have now won 2nd place in competitions - 'Digging' and 'Last Samaritan in Paris' - thank you to the editor of 'Country Living' magazine and to the team at *These3Streams Festival*. 'Revelation' won 1st prize in the *Aberystwyth Poetry Festival* competition 2023 - a welcome morale boost earlier this year.

Gratitude is also offered to The Dawntreader, Hedgehog Poetry and Black Bough who will all be publishing further new poems in the coming months...the beginnings of my next collection perhaps...

About *Bracing*...and about Simone

A collection of 55 poems, whose themes include climate change, climate as a lived experience, the frustrations and joys of being human, and female, in 2023, but the recent craziness of the pandemic too. Parenthood, mental illness, dementia, ageing, marriage, rural life, memories of family members, love, lust, small children, dogs, the death of pets, as well as contemporary experience viewed through the prism of myth, history and legend – the range of this collection is huge, human, accessible, angry, tender and wry.

For Simone Mansell Broome, coming back to Wales was never a 'whether' but always a 'when'. It took a very long time. Simone was born in Tenby. Her grandfather was a tenant farmer on Folly Farm in Pembrokeshire. She's descended from peasants, self-made and self-taught men, suffragists and Gunpowder plotters. Simone's an optimist, businesswoman, lover of both stage and page, and is passionate about the environment.

www.simonemansellbroome.com

More Testimonials

'Memories, fragments, forgotten moments, emotions and remembrances. From the first signs of spring to the '*so many chapels*' of her Wales and her own personal Hiraeth, Simone shows us humour and sadness in the everyday and the power of homesickness. *Bracing* is packed with hidden gems to make you laugh, cry and ponder on the past, present and future of our ever changing world.'

'I love the collection - I'm particularly fond of Hole Punch! Fabulous.'

Ann Fletcher-Williams, Artist

'Your scope of subject matter is so enjoyable as is the style in which you approach poems.'

'Here are poems of experience, anticipation and observation that share an engagement with life - for all its complexities; for all its failures, successes, tragedies and humour. Poems that seek and find reward in the commonness of everyday events. Poems that capture a reader's mind with their conversational style.'

Ric Hool, poet

These are quirky poems written from unusual angles, some comic, some sinister. Several were written during Covid, when we all felt desperate but when the poet's friend went out and became a cheerful land girl. We all die in the end, she says, but life is here to be celebrated. Bracing indeed!'

Merryn Williams, poet and editor